T0198586

BEING EMPOWERED BY THE KNOWLEDGE OF CHRIST

SHARAINA REED

BEING EMPOWERED BY THE KNOWLEDGE OF CHRIST

iUniverse books may be ordered through booksellers or by contacting:

iUniverse
1663 Liberty Drive
Bloomington, IN 47403
www.iuniverse.com
1-800-Authors (1-800-288-4677)

ISBN: 978-1-5320-9980-9 (sc)
ISBN: 978-1-5320-9979-3 (e)

Print information available on the last page.

iUniverse rev. date: 04/30/2020

INTRODUCTION

If you are looking to be informed with spiritual awareness and to grow to be all god has destined you to be in him please read along. In this book I'm going to explain the power of sin and the power of deception and how to come out of it and stay free from it through Christ.

I want to talk about the power of sin and its meaning as well as the power of deception and its meaning. Sin will have you as in a place of confinement, stuck, and can't move forward such as someone in prison. (**Sin**) an offense against religious or moral law, transgression of the law of god, an often serious short coming (**fault**).

Deception will have you focusing on things that's not important or believing things that's a lie.

(**Deception**) the act of causing someone to accept as true or valid what is false or invalid. Jesus says in Luke 4:18(KJV). The spirit of the lord is upon me because he hath anointed me to preach the gospel to the poor, he hath sent me to heal the broken hearted, to preach deliverance to the captives. Jesus came to set the captives free.

I know the question comes now well how do I become free from sin and deception. Jesus says repent and receive the gospel. How do I repent? What is repentance? Repent means to turn from sin and dedicate oneself to the amendment of one's life.

How do I receive the gospel? What is the gospel? The gospel is the good news, receive means to believe (**believe**) accept

something as true feel sure of the truth of. The good news is Jesus came and paid the price of sin by dying for the sins of the world the bible says for the joy was set before him he endured the cross. Hebrews 12:2(KJV).

Peter teaches the day of Pentecost repent and be baptized every one of you in the name of Jesus Christ for the remission of sins and ye shall receive the gift of the holy ghost Acts 2:38(KJV) (**Remission**) forgiveness, pardon, remittal penalty, punishment, retribution. God said that he will send us a comfortor that will abide with us forever. John 14:16(KJV) and I will pray the father and he shall give you another comfortor that he may abide with you forever. The Lord was speaking of the Holy Spirit that shall live in the hearts of his people. Amen.

How God desires to transform us from the world the bible says we were born and formed shaped in iniquity. (Iniquity) gross injustice, a wicked act or thing. The world desires to change us like the world but God has always had a plan to change us. Be not conformed to this world but be ye transformed by the renewing of your mind, that ye may prove what is that good and acceptable, and perfect, will of God. Romans 12:2(KJV)

I spoke on what sin is and the start on how to come out of sin and be free from the penalty of sin which by is accepting Christ Jesus our Lord.

(**Deception**) and why is it so important for us to know what it is and know to identify it because it will keep us from sin. Deception is powerful and can be very harmful to a person believer growing in Christ.

I would like to talk about tradition we all come from some form of traditional background to where things would be passed down through our families whether it be a favorite dish of food, or clothing that we wear or a practice of a particular festivity we partake in or just how we think on a daily basis these are traditions. Some may ask why is it important and what does it have to do with my belief in God and what does tradition mean (**tradition**) an inherited established or customary pattern of thought, action or behavior such as a religious practice or a social custom, the handing down of information beliefs and customs by word of mouth or by example from one generation to another without written instructions.

So now we have a clear understanding on what tradition is. The bible says beware lest any man spoil you through philosophy and vain deceit, after the tradition of men, after the rudiments of the world, and not after Christ Colossians 2:8(KJV)

I would like to explain the elements of sin it's an act of wrong doing such as stealing, lying, fornication, killing, Adultery, Alcoholism not loving one another, not loving God, idolatry.

I know some may wonder well what is exactly idolatry-idol. (**Idolatry**) extreme admiration love, or reverence of something or someone. An idol is abstaining anything meaning possessions that I don't need to live. Jesus says love not the things of the world. The lust of our flesh will pull us away from God. We as the people of God should not live a vain life meaning being a partaker of the things of the world which have no meaning (vain) having no real value, to no end without success or result.

God said be ye holy for I am holy, 1 Peter 1:16(KJV) because it is written be ye holy for I am holy. I am the Lord your holy one, the creator of Israel your king. Isaiah 43:15(KJV)

I remember me praying asking God what did holy means to him because I always here it being taught and preached on that God is holy and that we should be holy, for quite a while I begin to have my own mind and meaning of exactly what holiness was until I prayed, it reminds me of when king Solomon prayed for wisdom and knowledge to Rule over the people 2 Chronicles 1:9,10.This is what the Lord gave me holiness is a form of lifestyle, sacred, set apart from the rest, different from the rest. Amen.

Reflection:

_____

_____

_____

_____

_____

_____

_____

_____

_____

_____

_____

_____

_____

KEEPING THE FAITH

How do we keep the (**faith**) complete trust and confidence in someone or something. Two things that God loves is faith and worship, Jesus is attracted to the two. The bible says without faith it's impossible to please him. We need 100% faith for he that cometh to God must believe that he is and that he is a rewarder of them that diligently seek him. It's like having a cell phone that is dead or only a certain percentage on it, it's nothing like having a fully charge cell phone you know it would work much longer then a phone with low charge to it. Sometimes we look and wonder where is God at or where was God when we felt like we needed him the most in our lives but God was always and always will be before we looked to him he always had his eyes on us. He just was waiting to make his move. He seen our situation and was concerned about it. Psalms 34:4(KJV) I sought the Lord and he heard me and delivered me from all my fears. Amen

How do we get closer to our savior Jesus Christ? We are like a glass cup Jesus is our water we cannot get the water unless

we positon the cup to allow the water to be poured into it. We all know what amount of drink we would like to drink if we keep the glass there until desired amount is in.

When we are desiring a closer touch from Jesus we pray, we fast we read our bible, meditate listen to praise and worship music we do these things not because someone tells us we should but because we desire to be closer to our Saviour Jesus Christ in our time of prayer ask the Lord to send people to help build us up in faith in him. For everyone that asketh receiveth and he that seeketh findeth and to him that knocketh it shall be opened.

When God comes in your life he desires to wash us white as snow, he told the prophet Isaiah he would wash him white as snow, Isaiah 1:18(KJV).When we take bathing or showers daily it makes us feel refreshed and good outside and inwardly, the joy that comes when God washes us inwardly nothing can compare to it the feeling that God gives us.

Being washed by the word of God is every believer need just such as washing our body's naturally we all have to stay cleansed naturally so as spiritually the word will keep us clean daily by hearing it reading it or the holy spirit ministering it to us. We also have to receive it in our hearts. The bible says when you hear my word harden not your not your hearts.

Desiring more of God, desire is a longing a craving abeing serious about what we are going for in life this is the way it has to be in our Christian life, for there are many obstacles that get in the way of us fulfilling our desire and destiny in God. Psalms 37:4(KJV) delight thyself also in the Lord and he shall give thee the desires of thine heart.

Matthew 5:6(KJV), Blessed are they which do hunger and thirst after righteousness for they shall be filled.

Reflection:

_____

_____

_____

_____

_____

_____

_____

_____

_____

_____

_____

_____

_____

STAYING IN THE FAITH

In the beginning of the book I talked about (deception) and its meaning, how do we truly stay in the faith? The bible says the flesh is weak but the spirit is willing meaning the spirit is willing to guide us to all truth. The flesh will have us all over the place focusing on things that's not important and was never Gods will for us to focus on, Our flesh talks to us some of us just never took the time to listen and hear what its saying. Have you ever begin to have something you wanted to do or go get, whether it was important or unimportant you all of a sudden feel tired? It actually could be the other way around you thought of something you may need or want or even thought of something you wanted to accomplish and once you got it you felt like you didn't need or want that particular thing? Yes this is the flesh, the bible says the lust of the eye the lust of the flesh and the pride of life. A good man foot steps are ordered by God.

How do I stay in the faith? How do I stay rooted in Christ? Jesus said if you abide in me I will abide in you as the branch cannot bear fruit of itself except it abide in the vine no more

can ye except ye abide in me. I am the vine ye are the branches. He that abideith in me and I in him the same bringeth forth much fruit for without me ye can do nothing (**john**) 15,4-5. The key is we have to stay connected to Christ. I know some may say I do go to church you can still be disconnected from Christ the building is there to build us up and encourage us in the Lord.

Staying in the faith can help by prayer, fasting, listening to worship music (prayer) I know some may not understand the importance of knowing how to approach God in prayer it's very important for us to know how and what to say to God which is holy but merciful. God wants us to approach him as a little child. We should (**Anoit**) ourself before we pray (**Anoit**) our head with extra virgin olive oil, the oil is a symbol of the blood of Jesus its more of a covering Jesus says the way to my father is through me. Jesus disciples asked Jesus how should we pray and he gave them the proper way to pray found in Matthew chapter 6 verses 7-13(KJV). Fasting is another very important element with being a believer and following Christ when we fast it's a form of discipline self-denial that God requires us to live a life of, and Jesus said to them can the friends of the bridegroom mourn as long as the bridegroom is with them? But the days will come when the bridegroom will be taken away from them, and then they will fast. I know the question may come in our thoughts well how

do I fast, it's a form of self-denial going without meaning food spending time with God in his word without distractions the time of this can very God honors our sacrifices. Examples of time can be between 12am to 4pm or it can be for a few hours as long as we make sure we give God some time without distractions in between that time of self-denial God will honor it Reading the bible as well. Meditation means to think deeply on carefully about so yes reading Gods holy word and meditation on it is important. Amen

Worshipping listening to worship music is very uplifting because it allow us to take our mind off of ourself and focus on God and that alone makes us feel good within, God loves to be worshipped it pleases him.

The Key to true repentance

It takes correction to be redirected, Redirection is the key to true repentance repent means to turn away from correction means a change that rectifies an error or inaccuracy, Repentance is the way to salvation in someone life. (**Salvation**) means to save, help, in distress rescue, deliver, set free. Jesus says I came to seek and to save that which was lost. Luke 19:10(KJV)

Reflection:

THE CALL OF GOD TO RIGHTEOUSNESS

(**Righteousness**) acting in accord with divine or moral law free from guilt or sin. Morally right or justifiable a righteous decision.

Gods call is not based off who our parents are where we live, what we have of this world materialism what neighborhood we live in, what race (**ethnic**) we are. Being called to salvation, salvation means to be set free from. I would like to talk about what Gods will for us to be free from, Gods plan is to free us from where we come from and what we once knew a lot of things that we practice and do come from are man made traditions not Gods way of doing things. Jesus said you follow traditions of men. Mark 7:8(KJV), for laying aside the commandments of God, ye hold the tradition of men, as the washing of pots and cups and many other such like things ye do.

I would like to talk about man made tradition what we know to be holidays are pagan roots and was always forbidden by God. Christmas, Easter, Valentine's Day etc. all these are considered man made traditions. Jesus said I called you out of the world we don't have to feel like we are acknowledging Christ or pleasing him by (**Vain**) practices (**vain**) means producing no results : useless. God talks about pagan practices throughout the bible that's why it's so important to read Gods word.

God did give specific instructions on how we can remember him, and when he had given thanks he broke it and said this is my body which is for you do this in remembrance of me. And he took bread, and gave thanks, and brake it, and gave unto them saying this is my body which is given for you do this in remembrance of me. Likewise also the cup after the supper, saying this cup is the New Testament in my blood, which is shed for you. Luke 22:19 -20(KJV). This is called communion that we do at the time of resurrection day (**Passover**)

The fall of man (**Deception**) have always been a key reason that causes the fall of man. God told Adam what tree not to touch he was able to go to all other trees except for one, the tree of the knowledge of good and evil you shall not eat for in the day that you eat of it you shall surely die Genesis 2:17(NKJV). God always wanted us to choose to obey him

even evil may be around us and wrong doing is always before us, God said choose this day who we gone serve he didn't want it to be forced. He said if we love him we will keep his commandments John 14:15(KJV) God still had a plan to save us even though we messed up. Amen God wanted to give us a chance to make it right. God sent his son the savior the bible says he so loved the world he gave his only begotten son that whoever believes in him shall not perish but have eternal life John 3:16(KJV). God did not want it to be forced as it was after the fall of man when the law was put in place they would get stoned meaning murdered for breaking Gods laws. God wanted us to choose his ways and his laws freely by our love for Christ. The bible says for the joy was set before him he endured the cross Hebrews 12:2(KJV).When our savior died he became that tree again that was given to Adam and Eve free will to accept Christ or to deny him. Jesus says think not that I am come to destroy the law or the prophets I am not come to destroy but to fulfill Matthew 5 : 17(KJV), (fulfill) bring to completion or reality; achieve or realize (something desired, promised, or predicted).carry out (**a task, duty, or role**) as required, pledged or expected. So we see here God laws never changed from the beginning to now God said I changest not. The prince of this world (**Satan**) is a liar and the key to deception as he always been as well he lied to Eve and told her what won't happen and God said what will the wages of sin is deaf. We can refer to Gods commandments

throughout the bible Exodus 20 starting here. Jesus deaf put us back into fellowship with God as in gave us access to our father because we were cut off after the fall of man. I praise the Lord for our savior coming to save us. Amen

The two doors deception trys to enter by whether it be by the prince of this world (**Satan**) or the lust of our flesh. (**The heart**) the bible says to guard your heart out of it comes the issues of life. How do we guard our heart David said thy word have i hid in mine heart, that I might not sin against thee. Psalms 119:11(KJV).

(**The mind**) let this mind be in you which was also in Christ Jesus, so we have to have the mind of Christ which by reading and knowing Gods word for ourself it's always good to pray before reading the holy word we don't want to read the word and leave with our own understanding, the bible says with all thy getting get a understanding of his word. Amen

We have to become gate keepers of our soul, the windows of the soul are our (**eyes**) and (**ears**) Jesus said if the eyes are dark the whole body will be dark. But if thine eye be evil, thy whole body shall be full of darkness. If therefore the light that is in thee be darkness, how great is that darkness! Matthew 6:23(KJV). We should not watch anything on tv (**ears**) what we hear can affect how we view Gods and his word which is true cause we know there is no darkness in Christ. Music that

we listen to all gospel music does not edify Christ it should lead us to lifting Jesus up and him alone. Amen

Matthew 22:14(KJV) for many are called but few are chosen being chosen is the key to our salvation in Christ meaning being set free from being chosen by God is a very special call but it comes with lots of self-denial of the fleshly things and desires of this world.

A (**believer**) one who believes one who is persuaded of the truth or reality of some doctrine person or thing. (**Convert**) means to change whether it is a person who adopts a new belief or a changing action to turn around an object or ones thoughts on an idea, convert means to transform God desires to change us we have to decide are we being converted or just a believer ? The bible says demons believe and they tremble.

People I want you to always remember sin is connected to (**deception**) and truth is connected to (**holiness**) Be strong in the Lord and the power of his of his might (**Ephesians**) 6:10(KJV)

.

Reflection:

_____

_____

_____

_____

_____

_____

_____

_____

_____

_____

_____

_____

_____

Printed in the United States
By Bookmasters